FARM

A LEGO® ADVENTURE IN THE REAL WORLD

Let's get work and meet the animals!

■SCHOLASTIC

New York Toronto London Auckland
Sydney Mexico City New Delhi Hong Kong

Welcome, LEGO fans!

LEGO® minifigures show you the world in a unique nonfiction program.

This leveled reader is part of a program of LEGO® nonfiction books, with something for all the family, at every age and stage. LEGO nonfiction books have amazing facts, beautiful real-world photos, and minifigures everywhere, leading the fun and discovery.

To find out more about the books in the program, visit www.scholastic.com.

Leveled readers from Scholastic are designed to support your child's efforts to learn how to read at every age and stage.

LEVEL 1 READER

Beginning reader
Preschool–Grade 1
Sight words
Words to sound out
Simple sentences

LEVEL 2 READER

Developing reader
Grades 1–2
New vocabulary
Longer sentences

LEVEL 3 READER

Growing reader
Grades 1–3
Reading for inspiration and information

BUILD IT!
Check out the epic building ideas when you see me.

Hey! Can I have a ride? I need to get to the end of this book!

It's morning on the farm. What's happening today? Let's hop on the tractor and explore. Who's in the barn?

Most of the food you eat comes from farms. You're welcome!

I wanted to be a farmer, but it was too eggs-hausting!

Farms are busy places, with animals to feed and crops to grow.

BUILD IT!
Create your own farm. You'll need a house to live in and a barn for your animals to sleep in.

There are 2.2 million farms in the US.

My favorite farms are ones that grow carrots!

5

Cluck, cluck! Let's go to the chicken coop. The chicken has laid an egg! She lays four or five eggs a week—that's about 200 per year.

She's a
busy bird!

One trillion eggs
are eaten each year in
the world. I like mine
sunny-side up!

I always
have mine
scrambled!

Oink, oink! These little piglets are hungry! The mommy pig, or sow, feeds milk to her piglets. Pigs are really smart. They talk to each other using grunts and squeals.

Keep it down! Pigs can squeal nearly as loud as a jet!

Phew, it's hot today! I need to cool down.

Here! I'll help you. Pigs keep cool by rolling in mud.

Well, I'm cool, but now I need a shower . . .

It's milking time on the dairy farm. Milk keeps our bones and teeth strong.

In Russia, people used to drop a frog in a bucket of milk to keep it fresh.

Ribbit!

One cow can produce over 80 glasses of milk a day! That's a-moo-zing!

BUILD IT!
Build a huge tanker truck to keep the milk cool and take it to supermarkets.

The biggest milkshake ever was made in a tanker truck. It made 50,000 drinks!

Tara

Big animal farms are called ranches.
This one has more than 1,000 cows.
Cowboys and cowgirls use horses
to round them up.

Cows are fast moo-vers. They can run at 25 miles per hour (40 km/h).

I hope they don't get lost. This ranch is bigger than 1,000 soccer fields!

Cowboys and cowgirls use lassos to catch cows.

Yee-haw! Watch this. Bull's-eye!

Yikes! I think I need a bit more practice . . .

Watch the cute baby lambs leaping and bouncing in the field. Lambs can walk when they are a few minutes old.

Lambs know their mom's call in a field full of noisy sheep.

You're not my mommy!

They have thick woolly fleeces to keep them warm.

BUILD IT!
Build a barn for your sheep to sleep in when it's cold. Make it warm and cozy!

The lambs are all grown up and their fleeces are long and shaggy. Phew! It's too hot. It's time for a haircut.

Pweeeeee! I use whistles to tell my sheepdog what to do. Stop! You're a sheepdog, not a bird dog!

A sheepdog herds the sheep together.
The farmer cuts the fleece. The fleece
is then turned into wool.

The wool from one sheep can make eight sweaters or 50 pairs of socks.

Can you knit? My sweater and socks have holes in them.

Only a tractor can drive across bumpy, muddy fields. Huge wheels with knobby tires help grip the ground. Hold on tight, it's a bumpy ride!

Most tractors travel at around 25 miles per hour (40 km/h). Slow, but steady!

Woohoo! This car is FAST! Race you across the field!

This is the easiest race I've ever won!

Uh-oh, I guess I'm stuck in second place.

The biggest tractor tire is 58 LEGO minifigures high!

Tractors aren't fast, but they pull all kinds of useful farm machines. Plows make the soil ready for crops.

Plow

Sprayer

Baler

Trailer

Sprayers water crops. Balers collect crops in neat bundles.

BUILD IT!
Build a tractor and a farm machine for it to pull. Don't get stuck in the mud!

My tractor is strong enough to pull this trailer, even when it's full of heavy pigs!

Oink, oink!

21

Most of the plants you eat, such as wheat, rice, fruit, and vegetables grow on farms. These plants are called crops.

Corn is tasty! It's also used in cooking oil, paint, and soap!

Did you know that corn is actually a type of grass?

23

It's harvest time! Grain crops, such as wheat, need to be cut when they're ripe. A combine harvester cuts the crops and then removes the seeds (grain), the part we eat.

Later, this grain will be ground into flour for bread and cakes. I wish my combine harvester could bake cakes, too!

7636

5000

Combine harvesters cut at 7 miles per hour (11 km/h), but they do lots of jobs at once!

BUILD IT!

Design a farm vehicle. What can it do? How does it help the farmer?

Cozy! I'd love a nap!

The leftover stalks are useful, too. They're turned into straw for pets' beds.

Most fruit grows
best in hot countries.
These oranges are
ripe and ready
to be picked.

There are
over 7,000 different
types of apple.
Yummy!

Bananas grow in bunches. Guess how big the biggest one was.

OK, one banana, two bananas, three . . .

It was 473 bananas! I'll show you . . .

Bananas are the number one fruit crop in the world—100 billion of them are eaten every year. How many do you eat?

Farmers don't just grow things for us to eat. Cotton farms grow cotton to make fabric, oil, and animal feed.

Read all about it! Tree farms are the best because they give us wood and paper.

I like flower power. Flower farms are so colorful.

OLD

A one-acre
(4,047 m²) cotton
field can help
make 325 pairs
of jeans!

BUILD IT!
Design and build
your own farm.
What will you grow
on your farm?

Vroom!
The rubber for
my tires comes from
rubber tree farms.

Farms are
awesome! Many crops
are used to make
medicines.

Build a LEGO® farm!

Use your stickers to create
a fun day on the farm!

Farm words

barn
a farm building for animals to sleep in or used to store grain and machines

coop
a shelter where chickens can lay their eggs

crop
a plant that is grown on farms

dairy farm
a farm where cows are milked

fleece
a sheep's woolly covering

grain
seeds taken from plants that can be eaten

harvest
when ripe crops are cut and collected

ranch
a large farm, usually for animals, such as cows

ripe
ready to be harvested or eaten

sow
a female pig

stalk
the long, straight part of a crop that other smaller parts grow out of

tractor
a farm vehicle that can pull other machines, such as trailers

I love farms, but I'm a little scared of cows . . .

Don't be such a chicken!

31

Index

Credits

For the LEGO Group: Randi Kirsten Sørensen Licensing Assistant Manager; Peter Moorby Licensing Coordinator; Heidi K. Jensen Licensing Manager

Photos ©: cover top: Stepanyda/iStockphoto; cover cow: mihtiander/iStockphoto; back cover top background: SADLERC1/iStockphoto; cover center background: MaxyM/Shutterstock; cover bottom background: StanRohrer/iStockphoto; back cover center: GaryAlvis/iStockphoto; 1: taxzi/iStockphoto; 2-3 top: ands456/iStockphoto; 3 sheep: sponner/iStockphoto; 4-5 top background: Maksymowicz/iStockphoto; 4 top: stefann11/iStockphoto; 5 top: agmit/iStockphoto; 6-7 top: FiledIMAGE/iStockphoto; 6-7 bottom background: wuttichok/iStockphoto; 6 bottom: anna1311/iStockphoto; 7 top right: georgeclerk/iStockphoto; 8-9 top: hadynyah/iStockphoto; 8 farmhouse: Kenneth_Keifer/iStockphoto; 8-9 bottom: ChrisAt/iStockphoto; 8-9 fence: wuttichok/iStockphoto; 10-11: Roy Riley/Alamy Images; 12-13 background: AnnaGreen/iStockphoto; 13 bottom: johnnya123/iStockphoto; 14 lambs: Award/iStockphoto; 14-15 field: blew_i/iStockphoto; 15 bottom: agmit/iStockphoto; 16-17 top background: Bigandt_Photography/iStockphoto; 16 bottom: annaia/iStockphoto; 16-17 stone wall: ands456/iStockphoto; 17 top right: sponner/iStockphoto; 18-19: Rihardzz/Shutterstock; 20-21 top: oticki/iStockphoto; 20 center left: deyanarobova/iStockphoto; 20 bottom: valio84sl/iStockphoto; 20 center right: Nerthuz/iStockphoto; 22-23 background: oticki/iStockphoto; 22 trailer: zorandimzr/iStockphoto; 22 bottom right: stoonn/iStockphoto; 22 top: Shinyfamily/iStockphoto; 22 bottom left: Lezh/iStockphoto; 24-25 top background: ThomasLENNE/Shutterstock; 24-25 bottom background: Igor Strukov/Shutterstock; 25 top left: Malll Themd/Shutterstock; 26-27 background: apiguide/Shutterstock; 27 bottom right: aluxum/iStockphoto; 27 bottom left: loops7/iStockphoto; 28 center left: ithinksky/iStockphoto; 28 top left: PeteMuller/iStockphoto; 28-29 top background: Joobhead/iStockphoto; 29 jeans: Mehmet Hilmi Barcin/iStockphoto; 30 bottom left: anna1311/iStockphoto; 30-31 fence: wuttichok/iStockphoto; 30-31 top: stu99/iStockphoto.

All LEGO illustrations and stickers by Paul Lee

ISBN 978-1-338-21424-6

10 9 8 7 6 5 4 3 2   18 19 20 21 22

Printed in the U.S.A.   40
First edition, January 2018

This book is finished, but I still have plenty of jobs to do. See you next time!